T0197422

FLOWERS THAT SMILE

Henry's daughter

WestBow Press books may be ordered through booksellers or by contacting:

WestBow Press
A Division of Thomas Nelson & Zondervan
1663 Liberty Drive
Bloomington, IN 47403
www.westbowpress.com
844-714-3454

Interior Image Credit: Gail Jacalan

ISBN: 978-1-6642-6207-2 (sc)
ISBN: 978-1-6642-6208-9 (e)

Library of Congress Control Number: 2022905872

Print information available on the last page.

WestBow Press rev. date: 04/20/2022

WestBow
PRESS®
A DIVISION OF THOMAS NELSON
& ZONDERVAN

Once upon a time...there was a cute, freckle-faced little boy named Tyler... Tyler was 7 years old and lived in a quiet neighborhood with his parents and little brother. He was a sweet and kind little boy, always nice and polite to others. It was the first week of summer and each day after breakfast he went to visit Mrs. Smith, his neighbor next door. She was an elderly and very nice lady. She was happy and always smiling.

Tyler loved watching and helping her work in her garden. She made Tyler feel good and happy inside... she told him it makes her happy to see her flowers wake up and "smile' every morning. Mrs. Smith told Tyler the beautiful flowers are a gift from God. Tyler thought that was a great thing as he watched the pretty flowers wake up and then... WOW! It was true!!

her flowers do smile as they open up their faces to the sky! This went on all summer except Sunday mornings when Tyler went to Sunday school and church with his parents. Mrs. Smith also went to church on Sundays, and worked in her garden after church and lunch. Tyler enjoyed their talks and learned about Mrs. Smith's favorite things, God and Jesus and flowers. One Sunday Tyler had gone to church with his mom and dad and hurried through lunch so he could go visit with Mrs. Smith in her garden… she wasn't there.???? He waited for their morning visit the next day… Hmm ? no Mrs. Smith again…and then the next day…. a week went by…and still no Mrs. Smith.

Tyler had knocked on her door but no one answered. Tyler was sad and missed her. Then a lot of people were at her house... in dark clothes. He could feel in his heart something was wrong. Then his mother explained to him that Mrs. Smith had gone to heaven to be with the Lord and would not be back.

Tyler was very sad and continued to get up every morning... to look at her garden. He told his mom he missed Mrs. Smith. He noticed Mrs. Smith's husband was very sad... he didn't water her garden at all. Mrs. Smith's flowers that used to wake up and smile every day had died.

Tyler knew he wanted to do something to help, and then the idea hit him! He asked his mom to take him to the $ dollar store.

He had a little money saved and he bought a package of flower seeds, a large plastic seed tray and a bag of potting soil. He planted the seeds, watered them and watched them grow... every day he took care of them. He talked to them like he had seen Mrs. Smith do to her flowers. Tyler's flowers were beautiful and growing everyday... and he was very proud. Then it was time to plant them in Mrs. Smiths' garden where her other flowers had been.

Tyler was hard at work planting the flowers when Mr. Smith came out and asked him what he was doing. Tyler answered "Im planting flowers that smile like Mrs. Smith's… I miss her and this is all I can do to take away the sadness...to plant flowers so they can smile at you…"

Hearing this, his neighbor, Mr. Smith sat down and began to cry. He had forgotten how much Mrs. Smith loved the flowers in her garden and had told him many times..."be grateful for the flowers because they are one of God's gifts to us".

It took a child to show Mr. Smith why we should love the flowers and how they make us feel. He began to water the flowers and appreciate the garden and smiles that God gives us... Mr. Smith and Tyler water the flowers together now...

Tyler is glad Mr. Smith is happy again and that God gives us people and flowers to love. We need to water them...and watch them grow!

About the Author

Author is a Christian Licensed Marriage, Family and Child Therapist, now retired after 35+ yearsfull time work, a mother, grandmother and great grandmother. Each story has a moral value and encourages children to be kind and good to others.

The Pen name "Henry's Daughter" was created years ago when my father would listen to me telling bedtime stories to my children... he told me I should write down the stories that I create for the kids... long ago.

Printed in the United States
by Baker & Taylor Publisher Services